The Reflecl
of
ABBA ZOSIMAS
Monk of the Palestinian Desert

translated by
John Chryssavgis

SLG Press
Convent of the Incarnation
Fairacres Parker Street
Oxford OX4 1TB England
www.slgpress.co.uk

Reprinted 2019

ISBN 978 0 7283 0163 4
ISSN 0307-1405

Acknowledgement

The author gratefully acknowledges permission to publish in a separate edition with minor revisions *The Reflections of Abba Zosimas,* which first appeared in his book In *the Heart of the Desert: the Spirituality of the Desert Fathers and Mothers,* published by World Wisdom Books Inc. 2003.

The text of Zosimas's treatise is translated from the Greek edition of Monk Aygoustinos, *Abba Zosimas: Most Beneficial Chapters* (Jerusalem, 1913), 1–25, which originally appeared in *Nea Sion* 12 (1912). This publication has long been out of print, but a copy of it exists in the Library of St Gregory's House, Oxford, and I am grateful to Bishop Kallistos Ware for making it available. For the French edition, cf. *Enseignements des Pères du Désert* by L. Regnault (Bégrolles-en-Mauges: Abbaye de Bellefontaine, 1991).

J. C.

Introduction

One of the fascinating puzzles confronting scholars of early monasticism concerns the origin and development of *The Sayings of the Desert Fathers*. Just how and where were the *Apophthegmata* recorded and transmitted? Texts from this period reveal Palestine as a key region where these *Sayings* were collected and edited.[1] It was here that certain hermits and authors, who had either lived in or visited the desert of Egypt, migrated from the end of the fourth century.

Abba Silvanus settled with his disciples in Gerara during the early fifth century. Twenty-six sayings in the alphabetical collection alone are derived from this group of monks. Abba Isaiah of Scetis settled near Eleftheropolis, moving finally to Beit Daltha near Gaza some four miles from Thavatha toward the middle of the same century. There he remained for several decades, serving as a living example of the old Scetiote ascetic life until his death in 489.[2]

The late Fr Lucien Regnault has demonstrated how *The Sayings of the Desert Fathers*, in both their alphabetical and anonymous or systematic collections, are found in seminal texts of the time. Such texts include the *Life of Saint Melania the Younger*, attributed to her confidant and chaplain Gerontius, and dating to the middle of the fifth century; the *Life of Saint Euthymius*, written by Cyril of Scythopolis in the latter half of the sixth century; the *Reflections* of Zosimas, who founded a community in the first half of the sixth century; the *Correspondence* of Barsanuphius and John in the middle of that century; and the

---

[1] For a more detailed study, see J. Chryssavgis, *In the Heart of the Desert: the Spirituality of the Desert Fathers and Mothers* (Bloomington, IN: World Wisdom Books, 2003).

[2] More on Abba Isaiah in J. Chryssavgis and P. R. Penkett, *Abba Isaiah of Scetis: Ascetic Discourses* (Kalamazoo, MI: Cistercian Publications, 2002).

Works of their disciple Dorotheus toward the end of the sixth century.[3]

We are told by the author of the *Reflections,* that 'the blessed Zosimas always loved to read these *Sayings* all the time; they were almost like the air that he breathed'.[4] Indeed, this treatise makes numerous citations of the *Sayings,* implying perhaps that Zosimas may even have borrowed from existing written texts. Abba Zosimas senses that he is an integral part of the tradition of the Desert Fathers, that he has transplanted this tradition from the chosen land to an adopted land, and that he is obliged to keep the memory of that golden age alive in his new homeland. Zosimas also reveals having heard various sayings of the *Apophthegmata* from other contemporaries, which attests to the fact that these were widely known and possibly even accessible more or less everywhere in monastic circles of lower Palestine by the middle of the sixth century.

Zosimas's reference to 'the sayings of the holy elders'[5] is perhaps the earliest such characterization of the sayings with this specific title. Like *The Sayings of the Desert Fathers* themselves, these 'reflections' were spoken and not written down by Zosimas. In content and style, they very much resemble the *Ascetic Discourses* of Abba Isaiah of Scetis.

Zosimas himself flourished between 475 and 525, from the period just after the fourth Ecumenical Council (in. 451) until around the time of the great Gaza elders, Barsanuphius, John

---

[3] L. Regnault, 'Les *Apophthegmes des Pères* en Palestine aux Ve et Vie siecles,' *Irénikon* 54 (1981) 320-330. For a selection of the correspondence of Barsanuphius and John, see J. Chryssavgis, *Letters from the Desert* (NY: St. Vladimir's Seminary Press, 2003).
[4] See *Reflections* [below] XII, b.
[5] Cf. *Reflections,* ch. 12 (Avgoustinos edition, Jerusalem, 1913), 17. Also found in John Moschus, *Spiritual Meadow,* ch. 212, pp. 190-191 (PG 87: 31043105).

and Dorotheus.[6] He is mentioned several times by Dorotheus of Gaza, who knew him personally and visited him as his younger contemporary and compatriot. Dorotheus may in fact be the compiler of the *Reflections* of Abba Zosimas.

---

[6] Zosimas mentions a visit to the monastery of St Gerasimus, which was founded after 451, while Evagrius Scholasticus mentions in his *Ecclesiastical History* IV, 7 (PG 86: 2713-2717) that Zosimas predicted an earthquake that occurred in 525.

The Reflections of Abba Zosimas

I. On Detachment

a.   When he began, the blessed Abba Zosimas spoke in the following manner. First, he would make the sign of the cross over his mouth. He would say that when the divine Word became human He granted abundant grace to those who believed and who still believe in Him. For it is possible to believe even now, indeed even to begin from this day, if we so desire. After all, our desire depends on our free will with the co-operation also of grace. Thus it is possible for whoever so desires to regard the whole world as being nothing.

b.   Moreover, he would take whatever he could find—a nail or some thread, or anything else of insignificant value—and say: 'Who would ever fight or argue over this; or else, who would keep a grudge or be afflicted over this; unless it be some-one who has truly lost his mind? Therefore, a person of God who is progressing and advancing should consider the whole world as this nail, even if that person actually possesses the entire world. For, as I always like to say: It is not possessing something that is harmful, but being attached to it.

c.   'Who is ignorant of the fact that the human body is more precious than anything else that we may have? Then how is it that when circumstances demand we are ordered to despise it (Matt. 18:8)? If this is what happens with the body, how much more so does it apply to external matters? Just as it is not appropriate to disregard material things unnecessarily, for no reason at all, it is also not proper to throw oneself before death. For this would be foolishness. Rather, we are called to await the appropriate time, in order that we may be prepared.'

d.   He remembered the brother who owned some vegetables,[7] and used to say: 'Did he not sow the seed, or toil in labour, or plant and nurture their growth? Did he perhaps uproot them or throw them away? No. Yet he possessed these vegetables as if he did not in fact own them (I Cor. 7:30–31). He was not therefore worried when his elder, wishing to test him, began to destroy them. This appeared as nothing to him; instead, he concealed his feelings. Moreover, when one root remained, he said to his elder: Father, if you wish you may leave it so that we may share a meal. Then that holy elder understood that his disciple was genuinely a servant of God and not of the vegetables. So he told him: The Spirit of God has found rest upon you, brother. Now, if the brother had been attached to the vegetables, this would immediately have become apparent, because he would have been afflicted and troubled. Instead, he showed that he possessed them without actually owning them.'

e.   Abba Zosimas also used to say that the demons pay attention to these matters. In addition, if they notice someone not being attached to things, because they are neither afflicted nor troubled by them, then they know that such a person may walk on this earth but does not in fact have an earthly mentality.

II. i. On Enduring Insults

a.   Again, he used to say: 'There are different levels in people's desires. One person may desire something fervently, and that desire will be capable of leading that person to God at one moment; whereas another person will not reach that point in fifty years on account of a lukewarm desire.

---

[7] See *Apophthegmata*, Nau, no. 343.

b.　'When the demons notice that someone has been insulted or shamed or harmed or suffered something similar, and yet that person is sorry not so much for what has happened but for not being able to endure it courageously, then the demons are afraid of such a strong will. For they know that this person has touched upon the way of truth and has decided to walk in accordance with the commandments of God.'

ii. The Prayer of Pachomius

a.　Abba Zosimas would remember Saint Pachomius, whose elder brother cried out, saying: 'Stop being vainglorious!' This was because Pachomius wanted to expand the monastery as a result of the divine vision that he was granted.[8] Moreover, as it says, Pachomius felt moved to anger, and justifiably so; yet still he did not say anything in response. Instead, remaining in control of his heart, he descended on the following night into a small basement, and began to weep, praying thus: 'God, the fleshly mentality still remains in me and I still live according to the flesh. Woe is me! For I shall lose my life, as it is written (Rom. 8:12–13). Even after so much ascetic discipline and spiritual preparation, I am still moved to anger; even if it is with good reason. Have mercy on me, Lord, in order that I may not perish. If the enemy finds even the slightest part in me, unless you support me, I shall submit to him. For *if someone keeps your whole law, but fails in one point, then that person has become accountable for all of it* (James 2:10). In addition, I believe that if your abundant mercies assist me, I shall henceforth learn how to walk in the way of your saints, moving forward to those things, which lie before me (Phil. 3:13). For they appropriately put the enemy to shame. How shall I be able, Lord, to teach those whom you have called with me to choose this way of life,

---

[8] See the *Life of Pachomius*, ch. 15.

when I have not first conquered the enemy myself?' Having prayed in this manner, he remained there the whole night long, repeating the same words and weeping, until the next morning dawned. Indeed, from his sweat the soles of his feet became like clay. For it was summer and the place was extremely hot.

b.   And the blessed Abba Zosimas said in astonishment: 'Were not Pachomius's tears without limit? (Ps. 79:6). How could God not grant His gifts to such a will? As for me, I am convinced that during that night God granted to Pachomius everything for which he had asked, namely to be dead unto all things.'

III. Healing from Christ

a.   He also said: 'If someone perceives that another person has brought upon him affliction or harm or slander or any other evil, and in return he weaves thoughts against that other person, then he is actually conspiring against his own soul, just as if the demons were doing this. It is actually possible to bring this upon oneself. What do I mean by "weaving"? If you do not imagine the other person to be like a healer, then you are bringing upon yourself the greatest harm. Why do you say that the other person has caused you suffering? That person has actually brought you cleansing. Moreover, you should think of that person as a healer, sent to you by Christ. You ought to suffer for the sake of that person (Acts 9:16), and you should regard that person as your benefactor.

b.   'If you have not been alienated from evil, and do not wish to be alienated from it, then the Lord your God is not to blame for this. To suffer is quite appropriate for a soul that is unhealthy. Were you not unhealthy you would not be suffering. Therefore you owe your brother a favour; because it is through him that you have come to know your illness. You should accept whatever he offers you, as if it were healing medicine sent to you by Jesus. Yet, not only do you not express gratitude to him, but you even weave thoughts against your brother. What you are really saying to Jesus is that you do not wish to be healed by Him; you do not wish to receive His medicine; you prefer to decay in your wounds; and you wish to submit to the demons. What then can the Lord do? For, inasmuch as the Lord is good, He gave us His holy commandments in order to purge our evils by cauterizing and cleansing them. Therefore, anyone who wishes and longs to be healed is obliged to endure whatever the doctor offers in order to be delivered from the illness. Indeed, no patient is happy to suffer an amputation or cauterization or to be cleansed with an enema. Rather, every patient thinks about such things with disgust. Nonetheless, that same patient is convinced that it is impossible to be healed of his illness without these. He surrenders then to the doctor, knowing that in return for a little disgust, a great deal of healing will result for an unhealthy condition and chronic illness.

c.   'Someone who inflicts harm upon you represents the burning medicine of Jesus. If you endure that harm willingly, then you are healed of your greed; if you cannot endure it, then you are bringing harm to yourself. Do not blame your brother. Unfortunately we are tempted to forget to blame ourselves and instead of welcoming the medicine of Christ, we start weaving thoughts against those who are our benefactors, as if we were out of our minds.'

IV. On Temptation and Humiliation

a.   He used to say: 'Take away the thoughts, and no one can become holy. One who avoids a beneficial temptation is avoiding eternal life.' [9] One of the saints asked, *Who procured those crowns for the holy martyrs, except their persecutors? Who granted such great glory to Saint Stephen but they who stoned him?* In addition, he always used to quote the passage from Evagrius, *I do not blame those who accuse me, but rather I call them* my *benefactors.* [10] *Moreover, I do not despise the spiritual doctor, who brings the medicine of dishonour to the vainglorious soul. My fear is that it may be said about my soul, that: "We have healed Babylon, but it has not been healed"* (Jer. 28:9)' [11]

b.   He also said: 'Evagrius feared that he might be accused by Christ, who might tell him, "Evagrius, you were ill from vainglory, and I administered unto you the medicine of dishonour in order that you might be healed. Yet you were not healed." We should also know that no one tells us the truth so much as those people who blame us.'

c.   Abba Zosimas used to say: 'The Lord knows, as *the one who tests hearts and minds* (Ps. 7:10), that even if everyone praises and exalts all that I do, nevertheless this deserves blame, shame and scorn. If someone were to tell me, "You did such and such well", I would respond, "What good can I do?" No one lies so much as those people who praise and exalt me; and no one tells the truth so much as they who accuse and humiliate me, as I have already said. In fact even they are not telling the whole truth. For they have been able to see only a tiny part of the ocean of our wrongdoing. Otherwise they would have completely repudiated our soul, turning away from it as if from defilement, stench and some unclean spirit. Indeed, even if people could be transformed into words in order to insult us, I am certain that no one would be able properly to describe our

---

[9] *Sayings,* Antony 4-5
[10] Evagrius, *Letter* 52, ed. Frankenberg, 600-601.
[11] Ibid., *Letter* 51, 598-599.

dishonour. For everyone who insults and blames us only expresses a part and not the whole of what we are. If the righteous Job said: *I am full of shame* (Job 10:15)—and there is nothing more to add to that "fullness"—then what would we say when we are like an ocean of every evil? The devil has humiliated us with every sin, and we should be grateful for this humiliation. For those who are grateful for their humiliation crush the devil. As the holy Fathers have said, *When humility is lowered to the depths of Hades, then it is raised* up *to Heaven. And if pride is raised up to Heaven, then it is lowered to the depths of Hades.*[12]

d.   He also said: 'Who could ever persuade a humble person to weave thoughts against someone else? For no matter what a humble person suffers or hears, that person will see this as an opportunity to accept for himself insult and shame.'

e.   In addition, he used to recall how the priests once cast Abba Moses out of the sanctuary, saying: 'Get out, you Ethiopian'. Abba Moses began to rebuke himself, saying: 'Your skin is as black as ashes. You are not a man, so why should you be allowed to be among other men?'[13]

V. i. The Way of the Saints

a.   He also used to say: 'Whatever may happen to a humble person, that person turns toward prayer and considers everyone as a benefactor. However, we have deviated from the way of truth and the directions of the saints. Instead we seek to forge our own way according to our wicked desires. Nevertheless, what can be easier than to listen to that holy and practical teacher, Abba Ammonas, who says, *Pay close attention to yourself. Then, if someone should afflict you in any matter whatsoever, you will be silent. You will not say anything at all until your heart is*

---

[12] *Apophthegmata*, Nau no. 381.
[13] *Sayings*, Moses 3-4.

softened through unceasing prayer. Afterward, you are able to console your brother.'[14]

b.   'For a person that longs for the true and straight way will rebuke himself harshly when troubled by something like this. That person will always practise self-examination, saying to himself: My soul, why have you lost your mind? Why are you troubled like those who are insane? It is precisely this which indicates how unwell in fact you are. Had you been healthy, you would not have been troubled. Why do you neglect to blame yourself and begin accusing your brother for revealing to you your illness both in deed and in truth? Learn the commandments of Christ, *When He was abused, He did not return abuse; when He suffered, He did not threaten* (I Pet. 2:23). Listen to Him when He says, and when He shows us in reality, *I gave my back to those who struck me, and my cheeks to those who beat me. I did not hide my face from insult and spitting* (Is. 50:6). Yet you, wretched soul, just because of a single insult and dishonour, sit there and weave thousands of thoughts, ultimately conspiring against your own soul in the manner of the demons. After all, what more can a demon do to such a soul that the soul has not already done to itself? We see the cross of Christ, we read of His passion each day, of what He suffered for us. Yet we cannot endure the slightest insult. We have indeed deviated from the straight way.'

c.   He also said: 'Even if one were to live as long as Mathusala, and yet not travel this straight way which all of the saints have journeyed, namely the way of courageously enduring dishonour and harm, then such a person will advance neither a lot nor a little, but will simply end up wasting all those years.'

---

[14] Cf. *Patrologia Orientalis,* vol. 11, 466. Also Abba Isaiah, *Ascetic Discourses* 27.

ii. Amma Dionysia

a.   Again he said: 'When I was once with the blessed Dionysia, a brother asked her for some alms; and she gave him whatever she could. However, since he received less than he had asked for, he began to insult her, speaking improperly about her and about me. When she heard this she was hurt and sought to harm him. Therefore, on learning this, I said to her: What are you doing, conspiring against yourself? You are removing every virtue from your soul. For what is it that you worthily endure, by comparison with those things which Christ endured for you? I know, my lady, that you have distributed all your possessions as if they were worthless. Nevertheless, unless you acquire meekness, then you will be like a forger beating an iron nugget but producing no vessel.' He also told her: 'Saint Ignatius the God-bearer says, *I require meekness, through which all of the power of the prince of this age is abolished.*[15] The sign of abolishing this world is not being troubled when someone insults you.

b.   'There are times when someone will ignore large sums of money; nevertheless, when it comes to a small needle, one's attachment to it may cause one much trouble. Then the small needle replaces the large amount of money. Therefore, one becomes a slave of the needle, or the monastic cap, or the handkerchief, or the book, instead of being a servant of God.

c.   'It was well said once by a wise person that the soul has as many masters as it has passions. And again, the Apostle says, *People are slaves to whatever masters them* (II Pet. 2:19).'

d.   Upon hearing these words, Amma Dionysia was attentive and amazed. She replied, 'You will surely find the God for whom you long'. Then the blessed Zosimas added: 'The soul

---

[15] *Letter to the Trallians* IV, 2.

desires salvation. Yet, in also desiring and being preoccupied with vain matters, it seeks to avoid pain. Yet truly, it is not the commandments that are burdensome (I John 5:3), but only our evil desires. For we have become accustomed to despise everything, whether for fear of the sea or else for fear of thieves. Therefore we readily surrender, even if we know that we shall die after a few years. Nevertheless, even if only for the sake of living a little while longer, we are prepared to despise everything. Indeed, we consider ourselves fortunate if we lose everything but still save our lives from those thieves or from the sea. And whereas, prior to this, someone might have been obsessed about acquiring a small amount of money, now that same person eagerly overlooks everything for the sake of gaining even a little more of this temporary life. Why then do we not think in the same way about eternal life? Why is the fear of God, as one saint put it, not as valid as our fear of the sea?'

In order to illustrate this, the blessed Zosimas related the following story, which he had heard from others.

VI. The Story of the Stone-Carver

a.   Once upon a time a stone-carver,[16] whom they also call a gem-engraver because he possessed certain precious stones and diamonds, embarked on a ship together with his sons in order to travel for purposes of trade. It so happened that he providentially grew to admire one of the servants on the boat, who would attend to him, and the two shared meals together. One day, this particular servant overheard the sailors whispering and planning among themselves to throw the stone-carver overboard because of the precious stones that he possessed. So the servant, who was deeply saddened, came to the stone-carver in order to attend to him, as was his custom. The latter

---

[16] John Moschus, *Spiritual Meadow*, ch. 203 (PG 87: 3096).

asked him why he was sad that day, but the servant kept this to himself and did not respond at all. Therefore, the stone-carver asked him again, 'Please tell me, what is the matter with you?' Then the servant broke down in tears and told him, 'The sailors are conspiring against you in such and such a way'. The stone-carver said, 'Is this true?' The servant replied, 'Yes. That is what they have planned among themselves.' Then the stone-carver called his sons and told them, 'Whatever I tell you, do it without hesitation'. Then he spread out a sheet and began to say to them, 'Bring me the treasure boxes', and they did. The stone-carver began to lay out all of the gemstones. After spreading them out on the sheet, he began to say to himself: Is this what life is about? Am I to risk battling for my life in the seas for the sake of these? Am I about to die in a short while, without taking with me anything from this world? And he said to his sons, 'Empty everything into the sea'. On hearing his words, they cast everything into the sea. The sailors were astonished, but their conspiracy was thwarted.

b.   Moreover, the blessed Zosimas said: 'Let us consider how, as soon as this thought occurred to him, that stone-carver became a philosopher in both his actions and his words. And all this, simply in order to gain a little more of this life. He was, of course right in doing so. For he thought to himself: If I am to die, then what do I have to gain from these precious stones? Yet we are unable to endure even a little harm for the sake of Christ's commandments. If it is necessary to grieve at all, then we should grieve for the loss of that person who has harmed us, not for the loss of our possessions. For that person has done injustice to himself by being cast out of the heavenly kingdom. *Wrongdoers shall not inherit the kingdom of God* (I Cor. 6:9). As for you who have suffered injustice, the person who has wronged you has in fact procured life for you. It is indeed said, *Rejoice*

11

and be glad, for your reward is great in Heaven (Matt. 5:12). Yet instead of grieving over the loss of one of Christ's members, we sit and weave thoughts about corruptible and insignificant matters, which are easily lost and worth nothing. We are truly and rightly condemning ourselves.

c.   'In effect, God has placed us in an order of many members, which have Christ our God as their head, as the Apostle said: *Just as the body is one and has many members, and the head of all is Christ* (I Cor. 12:12). Therefore, when your brother afflicts you, he is hurting you like a hand or an eye that suffers from some illness. Yet even when we are in pain we do not cut off our hand and throw it away; nor do we pull out our eye, but consider the rejection of each of these as being a very serious matter. Instead we place on these members the sign of Christ, which is more precious than anything else, entreating the saints to pray for them, as well as offering our own fervent prayers to God on their behalf. In addition to this, we apply medication and plaster in order to heal the sore member.[17] Therefore in the same way that you pray for your eye or your hand to heal and no longer to hurt, you should also do that for your brother. Nevertheless, when we see the members of Christ hurt in this way, not only do we not grieve for them, but we even curse them. Truly, such conduct is appropriate for someone without any compassion.'

d.   He also used to say: 'A person who has acquired a compassionate heart or a sympathetic love first brings joy and benefit to himself, and then also to his neighbour. On the other hand, the converse also holds true; evil consumes and annihilates the person who possesses it. Such a person imagines doing harm to his neighbour, whether in matters of money or glory,

---

[17] Abba Dorotheus, *Instruction* VI, 77

or even bodily harm, although in so doing such a person is actually depriving himself of life.' He also used to quote the saying: *One who does not harm the soul does not harm any person.*[18]

VII. The Secret of Peace

a.   The blessed Abba Zosimas also used to say: 'Once someone said to me, "Abba, the commandments are numerous and the intellect is darkened when it considerswhich ones to keep and which ones not to keep". I responded: This should not trouble you. Rather, consider the following. When you are unattached to things, then you easily acquire virtue. And when you do not seek after things, you will not be mindful of wrong done to you.

b.   'How much labour does it require to pray for one's enemies? Do you need to plough the earth? Do you have to embark on a journey? Does it cost you any money? If you are grateful when you are dishonoured, then you have already become a disciple of the holy Apostles, who would go on their way rejoicing that they were being put to shame for the name of Christ. (Acts 5:41) Indeed, they endured this while they were clean and holy, simply for the name of Christ; whereas we deserve to be dishonored on account of our sins. In fact we are dishonoured even if no one shames and curses us: *You rebuke the insolent, accursed ones, who wander from your commandments* (Ps. 119:21). It is not appropriate for everyone to be dishonoured for the name of Christ; this belongs to the holy and pure ones, as I said before. As for us, however, it is appropriate to accept and confess with thanksgiving that we are rightly dishonoured on account of our evil deeds.

c.   'Nevertheless, our wretched soul, while being aware of its impure actions, and understanding that it deservedly suffers

---

[18] Unidentified saying.

whatever it suffers, sits back and falsely reasons with its own conscience, weaving thoughts and saying: 'Such and such spoke against me, and shamed me and insulted me'. In this way, the soul is conspiring against itself and substituting the demons. What we see happening in the crafts also happens in the art of the soul. For a master conveys a particular craft to a disciple and then allows the disciple to work on his own, no longer regarding it as necessary to sit beside the disciple but only on occasion paying a visit in order to see whether the disciple has neglected the craft or perhaps even lost it. In the same way, the demons that see the soul obeying and readily accepting evil thoughts surrender the soul to the demonic craft. They do not need to sit beside it all the time, knowing that the soul is sufficiently capable of conspiring against itself; they simply visit the soul from time to time in order to see whether it has neglected their craft.

d.   'What can be simpler than to love everyone and be loved by everyone? What great comfort do we not receive from the commandments of Christ? Nonetheless, our free will is not passionate enough.[19] If it were truly passionate, then by the grace of God everything would appear simple for our free will. As I have frequently told you, a small inclination of our desire is able to attract God for our assistance. Moreover, as the holy Antony says: *Virtue only requires our desire.* Or again: *We do not need to make a great journey in order to reach the heavenly kingdom, nor do we need to cross the seas in order to acquire virtue.*[20] What rest is lacking from the meek and humble person? Truly: *The meek*

---

[19] In this case, the word 'passionate' is used by Zosimas to show the intense desire that one is called to direct toward God. However, the term employed here is *orme* (or desire) and not *pathos* or (passion).
[20] *Life of Antony,* ch. 20.

shall inherit the land, and delight themselves in abundant prosperity (Ps. 37:11).'

VIII. Lessons on Humility

a.   Again, the blessed Abba Zosimas used to say: 'Once, a brother and I were travelling together with some lay people on the way to Neapolis, and we arrived at a place where there was a customs house. The lay people were familiar with the custom and paid their due. The brother who was with me started to object, saying, "How dare you demand money from monks?" When I heard this, I said to him: Brother, what are you doing? What you are actually saying here is, whether you like it or not, you should honour me as a holy person. It would have been preferable if that person recognized your good will and felt shamed by your humility, asking for your forgiveness. Therefore, as a disciple of the meek and humble one (Matt. 11:29), pay the toll and move on peacefully.

b.   'On another occasion, when I happened to be in the Holy City [of Jerusalem],[21] a Christian layman approached me and said: "My brother and I have had a slight argument, but he does not wish to be reconciled with me. Please exhort him by speaking to him." I was very glad to accept this request, and called the brother in order to speak to him about the meaning of love and peace. He seemed to be persuaded, but then he told me that he could not be reconciled with his brother because he had sworn by the cross. I smiled and told him: Your oath is like saying to Christ that, by His precious cross, you will not keep His commandments but instead prefer to perform the will of His enemy the devil. For not only are we not obliged to keep to something that was wrongly decided, but also we should rather repent and grieve over our wrong decision, as the God-bearing

---

[21] Moschus, *Spiritual Meadow*, ch. 216 (PG 87: 3108).

15

Basil states.[22] For indeed, had even Herod repented and not kept his oath, he would not have fallen into that great sin of beheading the Forerunner of Christ. Then I proceeded to quote for him the passage from Saint Basil, wherein he commented on the Gospel words that the Lord desired to wash the feet of Saint Peter, and the latter objected. (cf. John 13:1–11)'[23]

IX. On Spiritual Discipline

a.   The blessed Abba Zosimas also said: 'I was once asked how one should control one's anger. And I responded: The beginning of controlling one's anger is not speaking when one is troubled. This is why Abba Moses was not troubled, although he was despised by those who asked him: What are you doing among us, you Ethiopian? He simply said: *Although I was troubled, I did not speak* (Ps. 118:60). The second thing that Abba Moses did was not only to remain untroubled, but even to rebuke himself, saying, "Your skin is as black as ashes. You are not a man, so why should you be allowed to be among other people."[24]

b.   'We, however, are very much inferior to Abba Moses, for we cannot even attain to the beginner's stage on account of our great neglect; and so we think that these commandments are immense and impossible. For to be troubled and not to speak is not for those who are perfect, but for beginners. What is truly great is not to be troubled at all, according to the holy prophet who said: *I was put to shame, but was not troubled* (Ps. 118.60). Yet, we do not seek to make a beginning in this; nor again do we even show any desire toward it, in order to attract God's grace for our assistance. Indeed, even when we think we are

---

[22] *Letter* 199 *to Amphilochius*, ch. 29 (PG 32: 725).
[23] *Short Rules* 60 (PG 31: 1122). See also *On the Judgment of God* 7 (PG 32: 672).
[24] *Sayings,* Moses 3-4.

showing some desire, it is actually lukewarm and worthless, undeserving to receive anything good from God.

c.   'Everything that we do in the spiritual life is like the seed and the crop. We offer our free will, and we receive from grace. It is like the farmer who sows a little, but with God's pleasure reaps a great deal for his labour. As it is written about Isaac, *he sowed in that land and harvested barley one hundred-fold during that year* (Gen. 26:12). So also, if God blesses our free will, we are able to achieve everything dispassionately, effortlessly and comfortably. For making an effort to pray and to endure produces pure and comfortable prayer. Moreover, forcing our free will to act brings the action of grace comfortably.

d.   'We can see the same thing happening in every craft. For when someone approaches a master in order to learn a craft, at the beginning he toils and is clumsy, sometimes even destroying his work. Nevertheless, he is not discouraged by this, but simply tries again[25]. Even if the work is destroyed a second time, still he does not give in but shows the master his attempts. In fact, if he is discouraged and gives up, then he learns nothing at all. If he destroys the work many times but does not give up, instead persisting in his labour and work, then he will learn the technique with God's grace and will start doing everything easily and confidently, to the point where he may even make a living from it.

e.   'The same applies to spiritual work. If someone undertakes the task of acquiring virtue, he should not imagine that he might achieve this immediately; for this is impossible. Rather, he should make an effort and not give up if it does not work out, simply because he cannot achieve something. Instead, he should try again, just like someone who wants to learn a craft.

---

[25] Dorotheus, *Instruction* VIII, 94.

Moreover, by his being very patient and not being discouraged, God will recognize his labour of desire and grant that he be able to do everything effortlessly. This is what is meant by the words of Abba Moses: *The strength of those who wish to acquire the virtues lies in this: that should they fall, they do not lose heart but stand up and try again*[26]

X. On Avoiding Neglect and on Acquiring Grace

a.   He used to say: 'Every virtue requires labour and time and our desire, and above all God's co-operation. For if God does not co-operate with our free will then our struggle is in vain. It is like the farmer who cultivates and sows his land, but God does not rain on his seed.[27] Nevertheless, God's cooperation also requires our prayer and supplication. It is through these that we attract God's assistance for our support. If we neglect prayer, how will God ever recognize our work? Alternatively, how can He do so if we pray in a lukewarm fashion or in some lazy manner or if we are quickly discouraged? As I always say, then we do not deserve to receive anything at all. For God pays attention to our desire and grants His gifts in accordance with this.

b.   'Was not Abba Moses formerly a chief robber? Did he not do numerous sinful deeds? Did they not even drive him away from his patron because of his bad character? Yet since he approached his new life courageously as well as with such fervent desire, we have all seen what spiritual heights he reached so that he was numbered among the chosen servants of God, according to his biographer[28]

---

[26] In Abba Isaiah, *Ascetic Discourses* 16.
[27] Abba Dorotheus, *Instruction* XII, 135-136.
[28] Palladius, *Lausiac History*, ch. 19.

18

c.   'Yet in time, through neglect, we lose even the little fervour that we suppose we have in our ascetic renunciation. We become attached to useless, insignificant and entirely worthless matters, substituting these for the love of God and neighbour, appropriating material things as if they were our own or as if we had not received them from God. *What do you have that you did not receive? And if you received it, then why do you boast as if it were not a gift?'* (I Cor. 4:7).

d.   He also said: 'Is our Lord so poor that He cannot grant us every good in the same way as He rendered the holy Patriarchs wealthy? If only He truly saw us profiting from whatever He bestowed upon us, then He would do so. However, since He sees that we are harmed by the few and small gifts that He offers us because of our bad character, He therefore can no longer entrust us with too much, lest we be completely destroyed. For He is loving-kind. Indeed if He saw that we could profit by the little that we receive from Him, He could easily grant us much more, as I said. In any case, who was it that persuaded those people to throw the money before the feet of the holy Apostles (Acts 4:35, 37)? Yet, it is as I always say: Inasmuch as He is good, God has given us to profit from everything. However, we become attached to and misuse God's gifts; and so we turn these very same good gifts to destruction through our evil choice and are therefore harmed.'

e.   He frequently used to say: 'No one can harm a faithful soul. Rather, everything that such a soul may suffer is considered by it to be profitable. Whereas an unfaithful soul is condemned by its faithlessness, like a labourer who receives a reward for his toil. A faithful soul, which remains faithful throughout the labour and expects to be rewarded for its endurance, will receive great comfort. On the other hand, the unfaithful soul, which does not expect to receive the Lord's

19

reward, will find no consolation. So it simply sits and decays in its own thoughts, dwelling on whatever small matter occurs: "He said this to me". Or: "I will say this to him". That person bears grudges and imagines impossible matters which he very often cannot bring to fruition. For people cannot do whatever they imagine, but only what God allows them to do and for the reasons that God alone knows.

f.   'Often one endeavours to do some injustice to another person, but if God does not permit the injustice to happen the attempt is brought to. nothing. In that case, the intentions of the heart merely are being tested. How many people tried to hurt the holy Patriarchs, but these latter came to no harm because God did not permit this to happen. For it is written: *He allowed no one to oppress them; He rebuked kings on their account, saying, Do not touch my anointed ones; do my prophets no harm* (Ps. 104:14-15). Indeed, when He wants to reveal the measure of His power, He is even able to stir to compassion the hearts of the merciless. As it is written in the book of Daniel: *Now the Lord allowed Daniel to receive favour and compassion from the palace master* (Dan. 1:9).

g.   'Truly blessed is the soul that through its thirst for God is prepared to receive His gifts. For God will in no way abandon that soul, but will always support it even in those matters where, out of ignorance, the soul does not approach God. That wise man was right in saying: 'God protects a wise person'. How many times did Saul attempt to kill the blessed David? What did the former not try? What did he not scheme? Yet because the Lord protected David, every conspiracy of Saul was brought to nothing. Not only this, but Saul was even delivered into the hands of the holy David who actually spared him. (I Sam. 24) For David was neither embittered nor provoked by evil.'

h.   Someone asked Abba Zosimas: 'How can one be despised and abused by other people and yet not become angry?' He replied: 'If one considers oneself as being worthless, then one will not be troubled. As Abba Poemen said, *If you take little account of yourself, then you will have peace.*[29]

XI. The Patience of Abba Zosimas

a.   He used to say: 'One day, one of the brothers who lived with me and who received the monastic tonsure from me, and for this reason also received careful spiritual formation from me—for he was very sensitive, and I would make concessions to his weakness—told me, "My Abba, I love you very much". And I replied, I have yet to find someone who loves me as much as I love that person. Now you are saying that you love me, and I am convinced. However, if something happens which you do not like you will not have the same sentiment. Whereas I, no matter what I come to suffer from you, cannot be separated from your love by anything at all.

b.   'A short time passed, and I cannot remember what actually happened to that brother. However, he began to say many things against me, and I would hear that he even spoke shamelessly about me. Nevertheless, I would say to myself: This is the brandishing fire of Jesus, and it has been sent to me in order to heal my vainglorious soul. From such things, one may gain much profit, whereas we gain only harm from those who praise us. Truly, such a person is a benefactor. Moreover, I would remember that brother as being my doctor and benefactor. So I would tell my informants: He only knows my visible wrongdoings, and even those he does not know completely but only partly. As for the invisible wrongs, they are innumerable.

---

[29] *Sayings,* Poemen 81.

c.   'Then, sometime afterward, the brother met me in Caesarea. He approached me to greet me and to embrace me in the usual manner. I responded in the same way, as if nothing had occurred.[30] And although he had said all these things about me, whenever he would encounter me, he would always warmly greet me and I would not give him the slightest indication at all of any remaining sorrow, even though I would continue to hear about what he used to say.

d.   'Yet, one day, he fell down before me and held my legs, saying: "Forgive me, my Abba, for the Lord's sake; for I have said many terrible things against you". I embraced him warmly and told him in a humorous manner: Does your love remember telling me how much you loved me? Do you remember how I responded, that I had not yet found anyone who could love me as much as I loved that person? Do you recall my words that, if something should happen which you would not like, you might not have the same sentiment; whereas I, no matter what I would suffer from you, could never be separated from your love by anything at all? You may rest assured in your heart that nothing of what you have said has escaped me. I have heard everything concerning where and to whom you have spoken. I never once imagined that this was not the case. Nor did anyone persuade me to say anything evil against you. Rather, I would tell them that what my brother says is true, and he is speaking out of love for my sake. In addition, I would never forget you in my prayers. In fact, in order to give you some evidence of my love, once when I hurt my eye badly I remembered you and made the sign of the cross, saying, Lord Jesus Christ, heal me

---

[30] Pavlos Evergetinos adds: 'This happened not simply once or twice, but many times.' The Armenian text also reads: 'We would exchange friendly conversation for a long time.'

through my brother's prayers. And I was immediately healed. That is what I told the brother'[31]

e.   Often the blessed Abba Zosirnas would say: 'We human beings do not know how to be loved or how to be honoured. We have lost our sense of balance. For if someone endures his brother even a little, when the latter is angry or afflicted, then when that brother comes to his senses and recognizes how the other has endured him, he would give his own life for that person.'

XII. On Meekness and Patience in Affliction

a.   The blessed Abba Zosimas also remembered that some-one once told him of a very meek Old Man, saying that because of his great virtue and the wonders that he performed, the entire land regarded him as an angel of God. Therefore, one day, someone was incited by the enemy and came to insult that Old Man in the worst possible manner in the presence of every-one. The Old Man stood up and simply pointed to that person's mouth, saying: 'The grace of God is in your mouth, my brother'. The latter was further outraged and said: 'Sure, you wicked and hoary old glutton. You are just saying this in order to pretend to others that you are meek.' The Old Man responded: 'That is true, my brother; what you are saying is the truth'. After all this, it is said, someone else asked the Old Man: 'Good monk, were you not troubled just now?' He replied: 'No. In fact, I felt that my soul was being protected by Christ.' And the blessed Abba Zosimas added: 'It is true that one ought to give thanks for these things, and if one is indeed filled with passions, to regard such people as doctors who heal the

---

[31] Pavlos Evergetinos adds: 'From that time, the brother completely trusted in me and stopped speaking against me, instead esteeming and loving me greatly.'

wounds of the soul; and if one is dispassionate, one should regard them as benefactors who procure for us the heavenly kingdom.'[32]

b.   That blessed Abba Zosimas again used to say: 'When I was still in the monastery in Tyre, before I had left that place, a certain virtuous Old Man came to visit us.[33] We were reading *The Sayings of the Holy Fathers.*' For the blessed Zosimas always loved to read these *Sayings* all the time; they were almost like the air that he breathed. It is from these *Sayings* that he came to receive the fruit of every virtue. So he said the following: We came to the passage where an Old Man was robbed by thieves,[34] who said to him, "We have come to take everything in your cell", and he replied, "Children, take whatever you think you should take". So they took everything and departed, leaving behind a small sack. Then the Old Man, as it is written, took the sack and ran after the thieves, crying out to them: "Children, take also this, which you left behind in my cell." And they were so astonished at the guilelessness of the Old Man, that they returned everything to his cell, repented and said to one another, "Truly, this is a man of God!"

c.   'Therefore, when we read this passage, the visiting Old Man said to me: "Do you understand this saying, my dear Abba? It has been of great benefit to me." I asked him: How? He replied, "Once, when I was living in the region beside the Jordan, I read this passage and admired the Old Man, saying, Lord, make me worthy to follow in the footsteps of this man, since you counted me worthy to wear the same monastic habit. Thus while I still had this longing, two days later, behold,

---

[32] Abba Dorotheus, *Letter* IX, 194.

[33] John Moschus, *Spiritual Meadow*, ch. 212 (PG 87: 3104-3105).

[34] *Apophthegmata*, Nau no. 337.

thieves broke into my cell. So as they struck at the door and I understood that they were thieves, I said to myself, Thanks be to God! Behold, it is time to prove the fruit of my longing. I opened the door and received them with gladness; I lit a lamp and began to show them my possessions, telling them, Do not worry, I trust in the Lord, and I shall not conceal anything from you. They asked me, "Do you have any gold?" I replied, Yes, I do, I have three gold coins. And I opened the box before them, they took the gold and left peacefully.

'As for me', the blessed Abba said, 'I asked the Old Man in humour: Did the thieves return, like they did in the story of the other Old Man?' He replied immediately: "May God never allow this. I would not want this to happen, namely that they might return."'

d.   And Abba Zosimas concluded: 'Look at the longing and the readiness of that Old Man. Look at what he received as a result. Not only was he not grieved, but in fact he even rejoiced that he was made worthy of such good. Indeed, since I have remembered this story', Zosimas said, 'in telling you all that I have said, how by enduring our troubled brother just a little we can even gain his soul, I would also like to tell you a story that I heard from the blessed Abbot Sergius in Pedias.'

XIII. The Power of Gentleness

a.   He told the following story: Once, when we were travelling with a holy Old Man, we lost our way. Not knowing in which direction we were travelling, we found ourselves in a field that was sown and we trampled on some of the seed. When the farmer became aware of this—for he happened to be working there—he began to insult us greatly, saying angrily, 'What sort of monks are you? Do you suppose that you are afraid of God? If you held the fear of God before your eyes, you would not have done this.' So the holy man immediately told us that no one should speak at all. Instead, he replied with meekness, 'You are right, my child. If we possessed the fear of God, we would not have done this.' However, that man again insulted us angrily, and the Old Man once more replied, 'What you say is true; had we been monks, we would not have done this. Yet, for the Lord's sake, forgive us; for indeed we are at fault.' The farmer was surprised and came and threw himself before the Old Man's feet, saying, 'Forgive me, for the Lord's sake, and take me with you'. The blessed Sergius would conclude, 'That man truly followed us, and even came to wear the monastic habit'.

b. The blessed Abba Zosimas added: 'Look at what the meekness and good will of the saint were able to achieve, with God's grace, for the salvation of a person created in the image of God, which God desires more than thousands of worlds and riches.'

c. Once when I was visiting him, he told me: 'Read us a passage from Scripture'. Now, as I commenced to read from the book of Proverbs, I came to the passage where it is written: *Where there is an abundance of wood, the fire burns; and where there is no anger, quarrelling ceases* (Prov. 26:20).[35] So I asked him: 'What does this passage mean, Father?' He replied: 'The wood causes the fire to burn. For lack of wood, however, the fire will go out. So it is also with the causes of passions. If one cuts off these causes, then the passions are not active. For example, the causes of fornication are, as Abba Moses said, *eating and drinking excessively, too much sleep, being idle and jesting and chattering, embellishment of clothes*. And again, the causes of anger are, according to the same person, *giving and taking, doing*

---

[35] See Abba Dorotheus, *Instruction* VIII, 91.

one's own will, loving to teach, and considering oneself as being prudent.[36] Therefore, if one cuts these off, then the passions are weakened. This is what Abba Sisoes meant, when he responded to a brother's question about why the passions do not leave us. He said, *"Their tools, namely their causes, are still inside you. Give them their due pledge, and they will go"*[37]

d.   'A person of dissent, in whom quarrel is not calmed, is one who is never content with being troubled once but provokes himself to anger a second time. The opposite kind of person will come to himself when provoked to anger and will blame himself, approaching the brother against whom he was angered in order to repent. Such a one is not a person of dissent. For quarrel is calmed within this person. Such a one will accuse himself and be reconciled with his brother so that there will be no room for quarrel within, as I have already said. On the other hand, someone who is angry but does not blame himself prefers rather to be provoked to anger and regrets not so much the anger as such, but not having said more against his brother than what was already spoken in turmoil. Such a one is called a dissenter. In such a person quarrel is never calmed. For anger is succeeded by grudge, and sorrow, and evil. May the Lord Jesus Christ deliver us of this kind, and make us worthy to be with the meek and humble.'

e.   Abba Zosimas often used to say: 'We require great vigilance and much prudence in order to face the variety of the devil's evil. For there are times when the devil will cause someone to be troubled out of nothing; and there are other times when the devil will propose a reasonable excuse, in order that one may suppose that he was justly angered for a good reason. Nevertheless, for someone who truly longs to

---

[36] See Abba Isaiah, *Ascetic Discourses* 7
[37] *Sayings*, Sisoes 6. See also Abba Dorotheus, *Instruction* XIII, 141.

27

travel the way of the saints, this is completely foreign, as Saint Maearius says, *It is not proper for monks to become angry, just as it is inappropriate for monks to grieve their neighbour.*[38]

f.　　He also used to say: 'Once, I commissioned certain books from a brilliant calligrapher. When he had completed his work of writing, he sent me a message saying, "I have finished my work. Whenever you want, send someone to pick them up." When one of the brothers heard about this, he went to the calligrapher in my name, paid him the money and took the books. Since I was unaware of this, I sent one of our other brothers with a letter and the payment in order for the books to be picked up. Now when the calligrapher understood that he was deceived by the first brother, who had already picked them up, he was troubled and said, "Indeed, I am going to be disgusted with that brother in two ways: both because he tricked me, as well as because he took what did not belong to him." When I heard this, I sent him a message saying: My brother, you know that we acquire books in order to learn from them about love, humility and meekness. If the beginning of acquiring books includes a quarrel, then I do not want to acquire any books in order to start quarrelling: *The Lord's servant must not be quarrelsome* (II Tim. 2:24). Thus, by despising the book, I helped the brother not to be troubled at all.'

XIV. On the Subject of Spiritual Gain

a.　　The blessed Abba Zosimas used to sit down and talk on the subject of spiritual gain. He would begin by quoting some of the words of the holy Fathers. He came to the saying [in the *Apophthegmata*] by Abba Poemen, namely that *one who blames*

---

[38] Saying preserved in the Coptic: Am 171, 16 (*Sentences des Péres*, suppl. Solesmes, 1976) 176. See Dorotheus, *Instruction* II, 29 and VIII, 89, where he attributes this saying to Evagrius.

himself finds rest in everything.[39] He also came to the saying [in the *Apophthegmata*] by the Abba of the Nitrian mountain who was asked what more he had found in his particular way of living. He replied that he had learned to accuse and blame himself at all times, to which the person asking the question added: 'There is no other way but this'.[40] And Abba Zosimas would say: 'What power is contained in the words of the saints! Truly, whatever they said, they spoke out of experience and truth, as the sacred Antony also says,[41] *Their words were powerful because they spoke of what they practised; as one of the sages put it, May your life confirm your words!*[42]

b.   Abba Zosimas also used to relate the following story: During a brief stay at the monastery of Abba Gerasimus, there was a particular brother that I loved. As we were sitting one day and speaking on the subject of spiritual gain, I recalled these words by Abba Poemen and the other elder, and he said to me, 'I am experienced in the truth of these words and in the rest that they refer to. For, once, I had a deacon, who was a truly dear friend in the monastery, and for some reason, which I cannot remember now, he held me in suspicion in regard to some matter that caused him sorrow. Therefore he began to look sadly toward me. When I noticed him looking gloomy, I asked him the reason for this, and he told me: "You did such and such a thing". I was unaware of having done anything like this at all. Nevertheless, I began to offer him assurance in this regard. He said to me: "Forgive me, but I am not convinced". Then I departed for my cell and began to examine my heart as to whether I had done any such thing, but I could not find any-

---

[39] *Sayings*, Poemen 95 and 134. See Dorotheus, *Instruction* VII, 81.
[40] *Sayings*, Theophilus 1. See Dorotheus, *Instruction* VII, 81.
[41] *Life of Antony*, ch. 39.
[42] Moschus, *Spiritual Meadow*, ch. 219 (PG 87: 3109-3112).

thing. Afterward, I saw him holding the chalice in his hand, distributing Communion to the brothers; and I swore to him on the chalice that I was not conscious of doing anything of the kind. Still, he was not persuaded.

c.   'Coming once again to myself, I recalled these words of the holy Fathers. Indeed trusting in them, I gradually converted my thought and said to myself: The deacon loves me genuinely, and it is out of this love that he was moved to confide in me whatever his heart felt in my regard so that I might be vigilant and more careful from now on. Nevertheless, wretched soul, since you say that you have not done any such thing, you have in any case committed thousands of wrongs which you have already forgotten. Where are all those things which you did yesterday or ten days ago? Can you even remember them? Therefore you must have done this wrong too, just as you did those; and you must have forgotten about this too, just as you forgot about those. In this way, I disposed my heart to say that I truly did do this but had forgotten about it, just as I forgot about my former wrongdoings. Moreover, I began to give thanks to God and to the deacon. For through him the Lord made me worthy to recognize my error and to repent of it. Therefore, rising with these thoughts, I came to the deacon in order to repent and in order to thank him. And as I knocked on his door, he opened and first made a prostration before me, saying, "Forgive me, for I have been deceived by the demons, suspecting that you did that thing. In truth, however, God has assured me that you did nothing of the sort." And the brother added, 'He did not even permit me to assure him, but instead said, "It is not necessary".'

d.   The blessed Abba Zosimas also said: 'Such is genuine humility. It disposed the heart of the one who longed for it not only in order not to scandalize the deacon or be grieved toward

30

him, first for suspecting him and second for not being convinced by him when he tried to persuade him. Yet humility even made the heart ascribe the error to himself. In fact, what is more than this, it made the brother additionally give thanks to the other.'

Abba Zosimas added: 'Can you see what virtue does? Do you see how many degrees of progress it holds for the one who desires it? For, had he so wanted, he could have had thousands of excuses to act as a demon toward the deacon. Nevertheless, since he was disposed toward virtue, not only did he not grieve over what had happened, but he even thanked the deacon in addition; for virtue had seized his heart. So it is also with us. If we are in timely fashion and dispose our heart modestly in the seed-bed of meekness and humility, then the enemy will be unable to sow evil seeds in the heart. However, because the enemy finds our heart deserted by every good thought, and even finds us inciting ourselves toward evil, that is why he seizes these opportunities from us and fulfils his work so that what occurs is opposite to that which happens in the case of virtue. For when virtue sees the soul thirsting for salvation and cultivating good seeds, then it too fulfils its gifts because of the willingness of the soul.'

XV. On Perfect Detachment

a.   Once, Abba Zosimas remembered the saying about the Old Man who was robbed by his neighbouring brother. Instead of rebuking his brother, that Old Man began to work harder, thinking that the brother had need of these things.[43] Abba Zosimas admired the compassion of the saints, and also told the following story.

---

[43] *Apophthegmata*, Nau no. 339.

b.   Once, when I was at Pedias, an Abbot told me this story.[44] There was an Old Man who lived near our monastery and who had a very good soul. There was another brother who also lived nearby. When the Old Man was absent one day, that brother was tempted to open the Old Man's cell, enter inside, and take his vessels and books. So when the Old Man returned, he opened the door and, not finding his vessels, he went to announce this to the brother. However, he found his vessels still lying in the middle of the brother's cell; for the brother had not yet put them away. Not wishing to put the brother to shame or to rebuke him, he pretended that he had a stomach ache and went to relieve himself, allowing enough time for the brother to put away the vessels. Then the Old Man returned and began to speak with the brother on another subject. He did not rebuke the brother at all. After a few days, however, the Old Man's vessels were recognized, and the brother was taken to prison without the Old Man knowing anything about it. When he heard about the brother, namely that he was in prison, he was still unaware of the reason for which the brother was imprisoned. So he came to me, said the Abbot, for he would frequently visit us, and said: 'Please, be so kind as to give me some eggs and some church bread'. I asked him: Do you have visitors coming today? He said: 'Yes'. However, the Old Man wanted these in order to visit the prison and bring some consolation to the brother. Now, when he entered the prison, the brother fell to his feet and said: 'I am here on account of you, Abba. For I am the one who stole your vessels. Nevertheless, here, take your book; it is here. And take this clothing; it is yours.' The Old Man told him: 'Child, may your heart be assured that this is not the reason I came here. I did not know at all that you are here because of me. Nevertheless, on

---

[44] Moschus, *Spiritual Meadow*, ch. 211 (PG 87: 3101-3104).

hearing that you are here, I was saddened. Therefore I have come to bring you some consolation. Look, here are some eggs and some church bread. Now then, I shall do all that I can in order to have you removed from prison.' Indeed, the Old Man went off and begged certain dignitaries—for he was well known among them because of his virtue—and they arranged for the brother to come out of prison.

c.   Again, they also used to say the following about the same Old Man. Once he went to the market place in order to purchase some clothing for himself. And he bought it. Having given a piece of gold he still had to pay out some small change. So he took the clothing and placed it beneath him. While he was counting out the coins on the counter, someone came along and wanted to steal the clothing. The Old Man perceived this and understood what was happening. Yet, since he had a merciful and compassionate heart, he lifted himself up gradually, supposedly pretending to reach out over the counter in order to pay the coins. In this way, the other person was able to steal the clothing, and departed. The Old Man, however, did not rebuke him.

d.   And the blessed Abba Zosimas would conclude: 'How costly were the clothing and the vessels which the Old Man had lost! Yet his great will power revealed that he possessed these material things without any attachment to them. He ignored the fact that they had been stolen and simply remained the same person; he was neither saddened nor troubled. For as I always like to say, *It is not possessing something that is harmful, but being attached to it.* Even if this Old Man possessed the whole world, he would have done so without being attached to it. From his actions, he proved that he was free from everything.'

*** *** ***

33

Therefore brothers, let us too struggle to imitate with eagerness the words of the holy Fathers in order that we may bear fruit and inherit the eternal goods. In Christ Jesus our Lord, to whom be the glory and the power, together with the Father and the Holy Spirit, now and always, and to the ages of ages. Amen.[45]

---

[45] From the conclusion to the text (PG 78: 1701).

From the Teachings of Abba Dorotheus on Abba Zosimas

Once Abba Zosimas was speaking about humility.[46] A sophist happened to be there, listening to what Zosimas was saying, and he wanted to find out the exact meaning of his words. So he asked him: 'Tell me. How is it that you regard yourself as being a sinner? Do you not know that you are a saint? Do you not know that you have many virtues? Surely you can see how you practise the commandments! How can you do these things and yet regard yourself as being a sinner?' The Old Man could not find the proper way of wording his response. Nevertheless, he said: 'I do not know what to say to you in response. However, that is how I regard myself.' Therefore, the sophist argued with him, wanting to learn how this could be so. Yet the Old Man still could not find a way of explaining this to him, and began to respond with his holy simplicity: `Do not torment me; I just know that this is the case'.

When I noticed that the Old Man was unsure as to how to reply, I told him: 'Is it not the same, I wonder, in sophistry and medicine? When someone learns this art well and practises it, gradually, by exercising it, it becomes like a second nature to the doctor or the sophist. Then, such people cannot explain or express how this habit occurred gradually, as I said, and how imperceptibly it has seized their soul simply by practising the art. The same also happens in the case of humility. For from the keeping of the commandments, a certain habitual humility occurs, which cannot be explained in words.'

---

[46] In Abba Dorotheus, *Instruction* II, 36.

When Abba Zosimas heard this, he was pleased and immediately embraced me, saying: 'You are right. That is exactly how it is. It is just as you have said it.' The sophist too was satisfied with the response and admitted that this was the reason.

Abba Zosimas said,[47] 'Even if the devil, working together with all of his demons, puts into action all the machinations of his evil, all these strategies are in vain and are brought to nothing according to the command of Christ by humility.'

---

[47] Saying of Abba Zosimas, cited by Dorotheus, *Instruction* VIII, 94.